SUBVERSIVE MINDS
PENETRATING A SACRED
THOT

FRANKIE NICOLE

Copyright © 2023 Frankie Nicole.

All rights reserved. No part of this book may be reproduced, stored, or transmitted by any means—whether auditory, graphic, mechanical, or electronic—without written permission of both publisher and author, except in the case of brief excerpts used in critical articles and reviews. Unauthorized reproduction of any part of this work is illegal and is punishable by law.

ISBN: 979-8-88640-586-6 (sc)
ISBN: 979-8-88640-587-3 (hc)
ISBN: 979-8-88640-588-0 (e)

Because of the dynamic nature of the Internet, any web addresses or links contained in this book may have changed since publication and may no longer be valid. The views expressed in this work are solely those of the author and do not necessarily reflect the views of the publisher, and the publisher hereby disclaims any responsibility for them.

One Galleria Blvd., Suite 1900, Metairie, LA 70001
1-888-421-2397

Dear You,

This is for those who feel so deeply and dream long epic fantasies of love. Someone who never learned how to love themselves initially, so they look for it in everyone else. The fractured masculine and feminine within us all, fighting for a chance to be seen and loved. None of us can even claim to be perfect, that we haven't hurt or been hurt by someone. What we choose to do with those emotions is our choice, always having a choice in how to respond. I hope that you are always your first choice, that the first love you think of in the morning is yourself. It is easy to look outside of yourself for validation and hope someone has the key to what is right for you. This world is filled with so many paths, beliefs; choose what resonates for you.

Emotions are fluid and don't last, but the impact of how one feels can seem overwhelming and unrelenting at times. Not to be taken lightly or to mess around with. Holding compassion for yourself and tapping into the sensitivity of the state of your emotions is as vital as breathing air. Remembering this: not every emotion is good, clean or polished and some words might be triggering. This book is a subjective work of art, and it should be taken as such.

To those who have tried to show me love, but maybe it wasn't received well. I hope that you can understand that it wasn't about you, it took me a long time to get here myself. The empowerment of loving yourself after so many years of failed situations and destructive relationships. Drowned in substances and abusing the self not knowing that it was the wrong direction from what I truly wanted.

Life will never be a fairy tale, that's not what the message is. Love is a verb not a onetime proclamation. This book may be inked and printed, but the emotions that persist must be tamed and taken care of everyday. I hope you take this to heart and find a favorite passage, reading it when you find yourself lost in thought or anxious about who hasn't given you the time of day. You are worth every breath of air, every morning sunrise, the rain that falls to grow flowers and trees. Never give up on yourself or your dreams of finding the love you desire, but please I ask you to first find it within.

People may leave, they may abandon the dream you built together. It may seem like the end of the world some days but know that heart break only strengthens the resolve that your emotions are very real. Feel all the feelings to remind yourself that you are alive, here experiencing this reality. You chose to be here, so did I. We came to create beauty from an ugly place and that is true poetry.

Love,
Frankie

Contents

Chapter 1 Wounding 1
    Devil's Snare 2
    Dilation 3
    Death Becomes Her 5
    Cork Screwed 6
    Tart Eulogy 7
    Confusing the Waiting Game 9
    Blood Lust 10
    Bloody Entrails Dragging 11
    Death Becomes Him 12
    Last Thoughts 13
    Losing It 14
    Wandering Hands 15
    Enmeshment 16
    High Dive 17
    Inconceivable 19
    Nerves 20
    The Fear of Loss 22
    The Pulse 24

Chapter 2 Purgatory 27
    Dark Eternal Vibrations 28
    Implausible Dreams 29
    Expulsion 32
    Fucking Screaming 33
    Reconfiguring 35
    Infusion of the Heart 37
    Et. All 39
    Faintly 41

Chapter 3 Regrowth 43
    The Light 44
    Breaking the Black Hole 45

  Catch Me 46

  Soaring Hooves 47

  Thorns 49

  Crumbs 50

Chapter 4 Redemption **53**

  Trigger Points 54

  Oh! Goddess! 55

  Only Light 57

  Deemed Royalty 58

  Varnished Layers 59

  Low Point 62

  Glint 64

  Deftly the White Flag 65

Chapter 5 Inside Out **69**

  My Core 70

  The Mountain 71

  Sour Note 73

  Toxic Femininity 74

  Body Talk 77

  Perfect Timing 78

  The Consistent Question 81

  Taking Names 83

  Again 84

Chapter 6 Realizations **87**

  Pattern Breaker 88

  Ghosting 90

  Love Drunk 92

  Sealed with a Blade 94

  Sobering Up 96

  Done and Dusted 98

  Divine Surrender 100

Chapter 7 Secrets Grow in the Dark **103**

  Hidden Realms 104

  Maiden Voyage 106

- Switching Gears 108
- Becoming the Master 110
- Imposter Syndrome 113
- Difficult Maps 115
- Navigating by the Stars 117
- Releasing the Anchor 120
- New Horizons 122
- Promising Timelines 125
- Secret Islands 127
- Masters to Lead 129
- Dance Gods 130

Chapter 8   End of the Beginning 133
- Bye, Bye Bully 134
- Totaled 136
- Dismissed 138
- Indirect Directness 140
- Merging Two Wolves 142
- Reversions 144
- Shift of the Seasons 146
- Finding the End 148
- Baby Don't Hurt Me 150
- Karmic Block 152
- Free Range 153
- Disengage 155
- Fucking and Fighting 156
- The Release 158
- Expulsions 160
- The Truth 162

CHAPTER 1

Wounding

Devil's Snare

Temptation

All around

Much attention

To be found

I can touch and feel

But I know it isn't real

Powder fresh

Libations flows

Fresh growth of roses on a mound

Horned devils abound

But my thoughts only reflect of you

I wish you were here

I wish you were less stubborn

I wish I could always have my way

Sip my wine

Hoping to be fine

Cross my heart I'll keep my mind

Soon it'll be just us two

I promise I love only you

Dilation

Secrets, secrets
Lies
The eyes
They never lie

They may fib
They may skirt the line
Flash and spin
Flirt and dance about

But stare directly
And there is always truth

The wisdom
The knowledge
Of what is
What was
And what could be

The eyes that watch me
Veiled betwixt the sheets
I read everything in those eyes

Every flicker
Slowly
Explains it all

Are you looking at me?
I'm looking
I see

Do you see me
Or just through me
Am I transparent?

Flushing shade of chartreuse
When I show off my innards
Gory and gleaming

Screaming out loud
At the top of my lungs
Alone in gardens of my heart

Eyes
Shielded
Locked up to set free

Break me out of this cage
Flare in the dark forest
Tend to me with your stare

Those eyes

Death Becomes Her

She is stiff
Cold
No spirit
Waiting
To be put underground
There
The wasteland of her body
Nothing left to cherish
Next lifetime
You might have her
If you can find the one
That special one
That makes your heart go overboard
Beating out of the chest
Crying out in your sleep for her
For the one who makes sense
Who makes your soul yearn
You might know
If you really learned
But I don't know if you learned
I cannot teach
Had too many demanding pupils
You must feel it within
So again I say
Death becomes her
I shall return next time
For they have killed me
And now I must regenerate

Cork Screwed

Twisting and turning
My spine crunches as the bones go adrift
Spinning out of control
From where it supports my body
Turgot's of measly flesh that hold me together

If I do not allow myself to fly
Holding the truth within my teeth
Brandishing it all for those to see
How will they know?
Who will come to my funeral?
Thanking me for all those things I once said
The blindfolds ripped off from the bloody sockets
Painfully showing what was before unseen
A process of eliminating
The clutter and the crust
That destroys humanity
Tearing those apart that wish to be
All because of permeated lie
What do I say?
When you've spit in my face
Cursed my name in the center stage
Wishing others to see the lowest of my character.

Tart Eulogy

He calls me sweet.
Not endearing or literal like a cupcake
Or like my pussy, so good he can't take his lips away from.
But like:
"Aw you poor stupid, pathetic girl!"
Like my kindness is something to be ashamed of,
Like because I show vulnerability,
That somehow that makes me weak.
Shit, I've been bleeding monthly since I was twelve,
Who the fuck you think is weak?
Like because I don't right away point out all your flaws,
Malign any brave new idea,
Or take advantage of your need to feel a part of something
I must be soft…
Is my frailty showing, or just yours?
If you knew how many times I smiled instead of crying?
Those times when I wanted to slap someone for being such a creep,
When his hand moved far too close to private areas,
When the back door deal went to his buddy,
To be taken seriously as an artist,
But only 'sad faced' and raped.
It takes balls to be as strong as a woman
But balls are weak
So are those who subjugate with them
Turning around and torment those who don't put up an iron curtain.
Too afraid to embrace softness,
As patriarchy teaches them to kill anything nurturing.
So they do,
Inside themselves,
As well as in others.

With guns,
Available in all shades.
When they cannot,
They incarcerate.
There is a fine line between suspects and the real criminals,
Rocket man has to play a powerful game of swords.
My penis won't suffice, so here's some impressive CALORIMETRY!
You know what's sweet?
Kindness.
Persistence.
Patience.
Hope.
Optimism.
Somewhere we've lost virtues in the quest to impress,
Tired of this class slavery.
The serfdom that never left,
If the solution is as easy as looking within.
Assuaging our egos to take a moment,
Self-reflecting on why we are so afraid of our time here.
When we cycle lifetimes again and again.
Sometimes you are the clot,
Others, the artery.
Remembering someday dessert is served.

Confusing the Waiting Game

As she sat there perplexed by her current situation
Not knowing which way to go,
No moves left to make
Nothing but to sit there and wait.
Not a moment she was quite use to.
More like woman of action.
Stagnation was not a comfort level
She lacked a stable footing, her ground trembling beneath her usually stable feet
If she cried out for mercy who would answer the call?
Would she want someone to answer?
Could she afford the feeling of vulnerability?
Allowing another hand at the control panel.
To trigger hidden emotions that she dodged consistently.
What was she to do?
The idea to succumb to those feelings that could alter the beast of her being.
Too close to the primal heat and her fingertips might singe.
Blister up and tinge with the sharp pain of the physical plane.
That was real.
The pain, only a side effect of the excitement
Is abstract and cannot be caught up in earthy realities.
She didn't feel comfortable there,
How to behave and hold herself.
Indisposed, un-composed, like a contained symphony waiting to be written.

Blood Lust

Abandoned me again for foolish pride
I simmer alone
Yet, I am alright alone
Come to my peace with aloneness
We are alone in this life
From birth to death
I miss you though
To be object of your desire
The one your mind cannot release
A trap of neuronic synapses
Lighting up an EEG
I ache for you
If only I was next to you
My body lightly doused in the after glow
Waves of your energy flowing
You hurt me
Disconnected the chord
Shredded my spine
Left dangling dinner of wolves
Near death
For dearly departed
Why?
Why do you do me so wrong?
What have I done to deserve such a wrung?
Take the knife from my neck
Your wild look
That rings in your pupil
Is not from me
Blood gushing from the lips
I am not to blame
Please do not assert your blood lust on my psyche
Take the blade from my throat
Do not break me for the pains that others have brought you
Love me for I have shown you that you are loved

Bloody Entrails Dragging

I cannot give you hope
The pulse is weak
Self-fulfilling prophesy
Afforded you an extra life
From my own manifested
Price has been listed
Done what is done, DNR
Lacking what will with a bill
Depleted from the weight
Strong, but not carrying the both of us
Now only debt to be paid
Must find the strength to forge on
I only know my part
Come back, that is up to you
Misfortune and the blessing to see potential
Jump too quick then fall without a net
Only left is my shadow
Do they realize I have gotten away?

Death Becomes Him

Here on earth
We mere mortals
Exist as a reflection of the space gods
To experience who we are in different dimensions
To feel the connection of another human
To enjoy the simple pleasures
As the sad simple beings, we be
Pity us as you will but we pity you
Floating around with nothing and no one to hold on to
Pacifying your existence pulling the tendrils of others
Toying unconquered with lives
Never really living
Never really dying
Stuck suspended
To evolve is to die
As painful as it is.
Those brave enough to take a dip into depths of feelings
Welcomed with creatures and pathways unseen
You may think you know it all
Detached from the foolishness we vapid mortals enjoy
Yet, yet
That is the sting of the ego
Stunting your perpetual motion
Suffocating your dreams
Stifling your hopes
Magnifying your fears
Existence is to balance in between space and earth
Not avoid it like a coward
Reach for the stars
Not reside in mode
Your mortality is calling
Are you ready to die?

Last Thoughts

I realize my pain
Clouded judgement
Of what is true:
For the seed to grow
She must be willing
Willing to accept the task
He introduces to her
For he is the one who recognizes
A mirrored soul before him
However
Wherever the path leads
Must reconcile
Before she accepts her mission
Lighting up the world
With gold
Power and self
Raising the consciousness of others
Leading the way, they rein
She the expansion
The vessel
He the control
The initiator
Beloved they
Forever be
Combined together
Combusted in collision
Conquered hearts

My heart is ripped open.
Drowning in emotion.
It waits only for thee.
My sanctimonious broken king.
Feline's intuition.

Losing It

Don't give a hoot
Could not stop thinking of you with all my might
Underestimating the longing in my words?
Feel the fast-flourishing flush of my fire?
The needs, the wants.
Superficiality does not have weight here.
Frightening unknown as pieces of my soul exposed
Completely vulnerable
Read deeper
Reach deeper
Go deeper
Consume me before the flames of my yearning overwhelm
This gentle constitution of mine
Subdermal contact burns
I want your eyes to say yes
Then your lips
Only the best inspires the best of me
Following the heart's consent

Wandering Hands

Hands off
Hands on
Hands off

Where do they go
Found my body
Found the mother sprawled out

Taking it with you
When you leave
How I am possessed

Daemons inside
Outside in
Snipping pieces of me

Shake my spine
Ensconce me
Dreams made

Dreams lost
The sprites bright over my bed
Dangling, as if on strings

Twinkling in my eyes
Swirls trace the sulci of my hippocampus
Stiff as a board

Paralyzed
I want
No! I desire
Hands on

Enmeshment

Allowed himself to look at her face
Examined every little inch of it
From a bump to a grooved wrinkle
Small and insignificant
Yet leaving a marring
Seeing the significance of life
Times of sorrow
Times so high and bright
The only thing unseen
The numbness
An empty void
How often did that swallow her?
How often did she seek it?
An escape from reality
From the mundane and tragic
Yet so innocent
Who could know?
She didn't say much about her feelings
He looked
Peered into the dilated pupils
Searching
For any significant shred of hope
All he wanted was to know
Did she care?
Did she want him?
Did she love him?

High Dive

I find myself
On the cusp
Of something new

Daunting
Taunting
Into the unknown

Trepidations
Peer forward
Am I ready?

Leading into the wilderness
Abandonment
Of sanity

Am I prepared?
Survivalist packed?

Will I ever really be?
Always will have to be
Ultimately
Prepared
For an exception

I want
I want so bad it hurts
With ever cell of me
Screaming, yelling
Torn between safety and a free fall

Gut twisting unstoppable lightness of plunge

DO I DARE???
For love
The final frontier
Truly solemnity to trust another
Fully
With the hand, the hard
Heart
Pressed and squeezed
Pulled and stretched
Blead and emptied of what is, was, and would be
Sometimes
We look for a reason
Sometimes the reason, finds us

Reasonable
Reasonless
How to know
Hand over eyes
Once leg extended
I step

Inconceivable

It is
For us
To be together
Imaginary wistful wish
A fantasy of fantasies
Where I build myself
A magic bridge to your broken kingdom
Where sorrows of past heartaches do not exist
But that is
A paradox
Because lacking pain
Pleasure does not exist
Knowing that I can't have you now
Allows me the pleasure to love the very idea of you
Every kiss we haven't had
Every caress of tingling skin
I adore the memory
Unattainable
I have just the reality of hate and war
Love is the only antidote
Love
Love
Love
Is the answer
What is your question?

Nerves

My heart leaps into my chest every time I hear the door sway
My stomach churns as if a million creepy crawly things inhabit it
Nearly void of course
Twice
I don't mean to be cowardly
But loving you makes me weak
My knees
My elbows
Grounded when I am called
Am I ready?
Capable or culpable
Verbalize
Say my piece without falling to pieces
Waiting for the hour

Extended time and I fear you've abandoned me
My heart
Such the fragile heart
That took the leap and tried to believe
Is souring with each minute you are not here
You spurn me
You burn me
Real tears,
Not whimpering simple manipulations
The first real tears cried in a decade
Wounded grave and unimaginable depths
Recovery?
Burdens borne long time held
Not the bridge nor tunnel

To be more feral,
I would burn your forest pillage your village and destroy the kingdom
But I know the better thing is just to walk away.

Unlike any other, yet
Cheap and easy with my love
Presumptions have a great cost
I am lost
Sobbing
You have broken my heart
For that there is no cure

You do not own my power for it is only my own.
Lost vulnerability shared, now I am just
A ghost

The Fear of Loss

Not taking a step toward something
Something you've hoped for
Yet also fear the failure
Why though?
Does past predicate future action?
Repetitive behaviors lead us in a loop
The misconceptions of a misunderstanding
Standing still as the world changes around
What are you so afraid of?
What if we fail…. but what if we fly?
Made it this far
Seems as if we have resolve to fix the cracks with gold.
The heart
Quivering
Strong yet fragile
Tempestuous frontings for soft soul
Face to face with the possession of my own desires
Afraid to lose all of self
Into demonic possession.
I want so badly
To take a leap
Blindfolded stepping off the cliff
The death of many seem to make me brave
Thinking again, that I might not see your face
Feel the slow supple moves
Suck on your fingers.

Do you love me enough to step out from behind the wizard's curtain?
What if we only had today?
What if we only had the past?
Wasted it with petty quibbles?
I would rather spend the future with you
In a love nest
Time is not a virtue for all
We must act today
We must act now
Be brave, I promise to be too.
Adieu Mi Amore

The Pulse

What speaks this heart
When there is nothing left
When it has burst forth
Bloodied and beaten
Transformed
For the Danzig
Dressed in gilded curls
Not knowing
Now wanting
But needing
Every drop of pain
To push forward
Forth for the likes of love
Without salt in the wound
How does it grow
How does it know
Crown of leaves
Crown of thorns
All the same to me
If only to grasp for a second
that who swells my heart
Too large for my body
Making for an impossible target
Fickle strings plucked
Joyous and tragic all the same
As we die laying
Twisted
Extremities
Consisting as everlasting infinite
A passing moment of pleasure it gives us
Forever etched

CHAPTER 2

Purgatory

Dark Eternal Vibrations

Prince of darkness
Slithering snake!
Wormed your way through my heart
Leaving holes and putrid puss
Oh silly prince
Little do you know
I have no heart
It was already eaten
Not a delight for you to devour
A lost soul of sorts
Finding no root to grab
I am limitless
Limited
Took me by the throat
Waved me around
Limp bodied wafting flag
Untended flesh
At your whim, sir
Just here to look pretty
Thought you had me
But no one has me
I got them
Read them
I see to, become them?
'Tis the life in ethereal
I wish it wasn't so
I wish I could submit
But it will never be
So, I bid adieu
Adieu
Forever in my dream
You will be
Leader, oh a king you
A brazen rose queen, I
I love you,
Eternally.

Implausible Dreams

Dreamt you up so long ago
Waiting
Sighing
I've pined for you
I lost track in time
Lashing pain with hope
Lessons came to unground my doubt
A set up to undo unrealistic expectations

Brought me to you
Landed unpredictably in my lap
Calm and cool, collected
No walking anxiety with you
Just sitting together as ourselves
Heard the expression of heartfelt love for me
Indirect, yet knowing it was meant for me
I was taken back by the candid statement made
Last time someone stated it too soon, such a disaster
To think someone would say that so soon again,
Not sure I was ready
I was unlovable at the time,
Past wounds held barriers to present
Wanting to believe but finding the will out of reach
But one of us had to be strong, save the day
Dismayed thinking you had to save me
I am a stature of my own strength and influence
I don't know what gave me the strength
Carrying my lifeless body to the end of the journey
I couldn't stand not having you in my life
A power disadvantage of imposturous proportions
Yet the struggle ensued

Proclaim to me, deconstruct my neediness
Saving myself from loneliness,
Begging to know that we are loved.
You've been trying to tease me,
Driving me crazy
Coo-coo coco poofs
In the bag waiting for a hand
Like the floor is falling out from under me
Give me your undying commitment and devotion
So loud and proud
Give it all to me
Your time and attention,
High priority for someone of high honor
Lest the assholes demand your time and leave such misery

No longer can I keep things hidden
Forced hand to expose the depths of softest emotions
I've fought so hard to keep myself safe in the cocoon
To be vulnerable
This chance only comes around once in a lifetime
A catch, not to be put on a shelf or taken for granted
Unmatched connections must be recognized
Painting the moon and stars together
This is our lifetime
Shatter the mold and making the amazing happen.

We can go the distance
Half in tangible realities
Others fractured within the subtle feels
My twin and a soulmate
Could not be ashamed or embarrassed to say
But to reveal it?

My beautiful soul,
Relinquish the devil that binds
Ignite with me
Clean up the soul, I believe in you
I love you
I want only you
Can't live without anymore

Expulsion

Everything I once numbed
Now leaks out of me
When it was easier not to feel
I coated it with varnish to pretend it was so pretty
Which is why I hold on
Because I know how it feels to be hurt
By those you trust
We're all just looking for someone to care
Some are unfit for the job
We become self-reliant
Hoping to hold ourselves up
But what then, when it all becomes too much
Do we dance and drown our sorrows with frivolity?
Meaningless sexual trysts
With those who can't look us in the face tomorrow
Clinging to our friends until they must leave us
How to step over the walls?
Barricades of safety to ward off dark night predators
Trudging forward into the wilderness
For comfortable alone has become
Comfortably disconnected
Carefully distracted
Longing for the touch of that person who will wake you from a dream
Paddling in the deep pools of our subconscious mind
Not afraid to peer into the water
The boogie man is only as bad as the unknown characters he plays
Can they keep me from drowning?
Or will they push my head under and swim away?
To revive love there must be clarity
For how many of us swim in the dark
Can I trust you to help me saw off this anchor?
Every human for themselves, then?
Fool me once
Fool me twice
Shame, shame, shame on me.

Fucking Screaming

I loathe this feeling
The lack of control I have
My heart like a floundering guppy
Tossed up on to the shore
    Gasping
So much movement
Too quick for the jellied candy heart of mine
Comforted by a large shell
Forced to find itself a new abode
How quickly?
On quicksand
With no bottom
And the drop
I need security
A handle to clutch
Subtle manipulations that carry the reins I am so comfortable holding
Like ripping off skin
Raw and blotched bloody
    I shiver
    Not just lightly
    A violent shudder arose to shake the soul
    Jaw clenched
    Blacked out
    Swirling, swirling
    If I hate this does it conversely mean I love it?
    Or am I just overturned in the surf
    Gasping for air

Mixed up in the cruel tricks of puppetry and slide of hand
Get your hand out of me
I am not here to play
Rules and boundaries, are you not following?
I did not take a fall because I enjoy scraped knees
Showing that I too, am human
  An air of vulnerability
  For arms to fold around me
  Hearts to reach out
  That I bleed the same too

Reconfiguring

You want to be a work of art?
I will take that as a yes
When you try to play my heart
Pretending until the end
Amusing playthings
Lovers for a night
Whether in my daydreams
Or deep in rem sleep tonight
Not so obvious
But deeply in the ephemeral
Repetitions, when and how
A mask of attentiveness
A fated fatal attraction if you must
Looking at me as he licks his lips
A magnet between our bodies
You see how conflicted yet keen I become
In your presence I am weak in the knees
Soft in the throat
So, I whispered silently in my head
Through my eyes I shoot my shot
Helps when the peanuts squawk louder
I am stealth
Sweet secrets and hot sheets
Snatched the sweet cream of the crop
Words like a vampire sucking blood
From your femoral vein
Circulating spiritually above your body
Like nightmares of the sweetest dream
Projecting confidence unto the wanting mouth

Feed me
The cries of baby chicks
Mewing mad cats
Roaring dragons clinging to gold
Beware my pointed arrow
She stands firm steady hand
Obey or die.
You may live with one exception
Amend
Grovel
Show me your humility
As quick as a beckoning eye
Freezes you to stone
Punishment isn't even enough
You coward!
As she rips off his head with her bare teeth
The same used to bite and bruise
The truth may sting
But deranged?
I do believe you are mistaking me
For a bitch who gives a damn.

Infusion of the Heart

Can you feel my heart?
It lights up with heat
Infused by a sober breath

Essence danced slowly
Tracing my skin barrier

A pulse heightens
Like those primal organs
Leaping into the throat

Dreary days return
In your absence

The rain rips open
Pockets of the skies
Pouring down tragic tears

The barometer stands
Lower than most
Dreams, Fantasies
Dividing me into two

With the strength
In my passions I am raw

Like liquid that escapes
Invisible cracks

Dripping slowly to the floor
A hazardous goo
Endangering those who
Remain unaware

I yearn
I mew
I falter
I fawn

To love is to die slowly
One million times over

Cells of skin that aid
Regeneration
The hearts electric connection
Peels me away slowly

Rendering all docile and still
I love to die every time you are near

Et. All

I want it all
The good, divine, and exquisite
The bad, mundane, and everyday
The ugly, vile, putrid and rotting

Should anyone steal that from me
Surely, I would die
My heart would seize up
Crumble out of my body
I would fall shriveled and dead before ever hitting the ground

A brief yet thorough haunting
This time I'll just leave
From the bottom up, begin again
Until the next lifetimes in formation
Meet me again, to have this love on replay
Rejoin the opposition of souls

I know you want me, all of me.
An inkling of intuitive nudges
Reflection of a soul so alike genuinely
The search just as thorough as mine
Desire to meet your match just as strong
Chord connected deep from your heart to mine

Chains cannot be dismantled
Bonds not broken
Love is on the table
Pull up a seat

Like a misted rose
Blossomed and at the precipice of its peak
I will not pluck you from the ground and keep you
Nor you will with I
For the spirit will die prematurely
No, no
I will grow beside you
We will grow together

My best friend, lover
Always in my heart

Faintly

Softly
Sturdy
Take it slow
Take your time
One beat after another
Patiently
Find me waiting there
At a crossroads
Left
Right
Right
Left
Crossing the boundaries of illusion and control
One step closer
One step back
Finding the wholeness
Was here all along
Be silent my sweet
For nothing says it all
The universe speaks
With the glory for timing
The beauty in small
The pause
The halt
Sweetness only abides by the rules

CHAPTER 3

Regrowth

The Light

I can see you
Transduced between layers
Peeled back
Sliced away the noise
Turbulent vibrations that distract
The pine of pines
Fresh green and fertile
New growth leaks out of every crack
Meshed and mixed
Germinated from the multitude of seeds
Effervescing illumination
The rest of the world waits for me to impress them
But you see I just am
Impressive
Expanding
Loving
Pure
Without presence
My special gift

Breaking the Black Hole

My heart, my heart
Love of all my lifetimes
Saving it all just for you
Every lesson I've learned
Every experience I felt
Prepared me to meet you now
Just as through your life
Has and will
Prepare you for
the gloriousness that is me
Together we will make magic
Glorious musical ingenuity
Greater than anyone has ever promised before
Because we know
And have known
What it is
The eyes, they never lie
My sweet, my dear my love
Just some time longer
Until I get to hold you in my arms
When the cosmos collide
A supernova
The reverb will be felt for millennia to come

Catch Me

The distance
Traveled
By me
Is not in question
I've been here in the background
Waiting for you
Helping you
Secretly
Playing those games, we play
Passing time to keep in touch
Rock the boat
We claim so innocent
With pushing boundary lines
Pop off of sparks
To tease or tempt a move
All leading to
A path we don't know the end of
But it seems
That we want to do it together.
So, tell me
Is that your goal?
Seeking answers?
To the end of all time?
As long as it takes, I figure

Soaring Hooves

My enduring love, oh lover
Followed by phantoms
Do not avert me my love
Find me
Face to face
Cheek to cheek
Ignite the small bumps of flesh
That are stimulated by the softest touch
Peel the droplets of sweat off my skin with your tongue
Vein by vein
Counted
All are plumped and erect
Pulsing
Soaring
Blood percolating a million cells a minute
Oxygen transferred into energy
Breath quickens
Beats tricky
Off and on
On and off
As if they were controlled by a short switch
I am no longer in control
Swimming
Mewing
Mailing
Misaligned
Flushed with a fever
Heat waves rise off pounds of me
Lost within
No longer present

Lover, oh friend
Build me a tower to peer over all
Will you invite me to join you?
Over air waves
Among trees
Riding through the night
Weary and lone
Communing
Vibrating in the ear
Input will return
Another screen and I will scream
Touch, I must be touched
Onward ride I must
Heavy handed and caught throat
Enough is enough
Even fools find a different journey

Lifetime to a space in time
Grand scheme of it all
Appears answers
Sat in trepidation
Knowing if I must
Seeker of the finer touch
Wasting time in the waiting line
Is it ever really wasted?
No real connection
To whom I speak
Emptiness becomes the weight of the world rested upon me
No longer abide on the emptiness
I must fill this cup
I will fill this cup
Hope fills up this cup

Thorns

The roses
Oh the roses
Neither you nor I own the roses
They do not connect us per se
It is a happenstance
That I am the queen of thorns
And you wear them around your heart
Thus is not us a couple made
Tragically
Romeo thinks Juliet is dead
Departs ignorantly thinking there is nothing left
She, transformed into someone who determinedly knows
How to handle the intense emotions in the flow
Direct her magic
Her projections of adoration to her beloved
Love only in the mind of she
Everything given is a reflection of her love for herself
Only a similar understanding
Symbiotically joining with that what she wishes to project
Hatred, shame, sorrow disconnects that which could have been joyous
For how long?
Who knows
This we do know
That each person has a path to traverse
So until then
My friend
Oh secret lover
An old reflection
Refract away the angles of disturbance
Untangle from my soul
Find me anew
Rebirthed
Returned

Crumbs

Loving someone
Let it be
The power of it all
Anxious quibbling
Grabbing
Consuming
Draining
Lenny
Mouse in hand
Being ever so
Vulnerable
Despite which position
Here we are
Can't say what I want to
Forgot it's not allowed
Only good for the dance
Pay attention?
What if
What if you don't
What if it doesn't
I know why
Stigmatized
Friendliest zoned
Blank place
Wasted
Feeling used
OH my feelings
Were really never anyone else's
Gotta learn
Don't hurt your own feelings
Silently
I hold on

Whatever the manufactured dream
Dreamt so many dreams
But really love
Not my religion
Way of life
No deity to kiss ass
No people to hate
Not even ignorance
I tried
Better to be compassionate
And let them fall
On their own dumbass sword
All goal posts on a different timeline swirling throughout space
I'm worried I might lose you
Again
I might be too picky
Unrealistic
Not nice
Overbearingly smothering
Mask that I wear
Unprotected
You from me
The annoying imperfections
Making me unlovable
Circle back into desperation
Heaving hard or makes the thread unravel
Instead of wrapped in warmth
Naked and exposed
Next to a clump of material
So hard to be vulnerable
With such an easy target
I tiptoe in pieces
Crumbs
Match your cadence
Because I'm afraid
I'll be holding my end
All alone.

CHAPTER 4

Redemption

Trigger Points

My dear sensitive soul
Take the brunt of my words too deep
Stirred within my heart a cauldron that needs a steady warm hand
Beholden by a firm grip of soulful scruff
Found the right angle
Your creative mind has too much freedom to roam into the darkness
I am the flame to glow in the blackest of nights
Breathe me in I will illuminate your world
Take the blinds off and you will see the warmth all around you
Do not sit in judgment of yourself
We all make mistakes
A slighted heart can have a sharp tongue
Pain from previously tainted love pushes a true beloved away
Longing to bury the head into chest, to be held once again
An unhuman desire that takes a hold of my entire being
Not to be shaken for hell or high water

Oh! Goddess!

Oh goddess
What am I to do?
I've lost control
Mesmerized by you
Lawd!
Boy got a hold on me
Don't know how to tell you
So I keep it on the low
Becoming harder
Not to love you
But maybe it's
Just a little crush
Obsessions
Come easy to me
The low lights
Keeps not all sights to be seen
Rush
Oh just a little rush
Of blood to my hushh..
Keep it all covered up
But I can't stop
With just a little touch
Sending me on a quaking spine
Might just have to make you mine
Under neath the glow
Moonlight view
Though I keep my cool
Wish you would make a move

In bed all day
Cuddled next to you
Order Chinese food
Get freaky
Big daddy one day
Soft kitty tomorrow
Let's play
Endless possibilities
With my mate
Best friend
Homeslice
Partner and in crime

Only Light

Shadows of night
I peer curiously over
Not everything is clear
But I can feel it
The tension in the room
So potent I can taste it
Who moves first?
A standoff
Between lovers
And friends
I don't need you
But I want you to want me
There's a brick in my chest
Welling with such melancholy
Pursue one's fear
Find what you desire
Open myself up
In the most intimate way
Because here I am
Showing that
Vulnerability
Stretch of the neck
So close you can feel
The beating pulses
That which reminds us
We're alive
Here to divide and multiply
Little parts of who we are
At any given place and time
The question is
Do I trust you enough?
To put my whole body in the lion's mouth
Do I?

Deemed Royalty

King, oh my king
Honorable, just and kind
Thoroughly all that you are
Leader of man
Master of just the one
Keeper of miserable misers and knaves
I do not place my own judgment on your choices
Beauty is pure
Love, respect and honesty
In equal exchange.
Malicious, unkind, unwelcome in this bond
Connection persists without touch or proximity
Pleasures free from toxicity
Only love and joy
Forever changing, harmonious alchemy of fire and water.
Steamy, reactive, and exciting
Stirring the animal nature within
My heart, not just an organ of flesh and blood
But the vessel of which my desire emanates
Cool, calm, soft, enveloping
Elemental purity of the combustion that with each beat continues the life force allowing it
Hot, searing streams of energy travel through each vein, vessel and artery.
Distinguishing it, life from death itself
Falling back into consciousness energy translates to though emoting frequencies that are received
You receive me.
I receive you.
My Royal.
And I be your Royal.

Varnished Layers

Who am I supposed to be?
Unbecoming, what is expected
So easy to just conform
Stuff myself into some low-rise jeans
Well, he likes it when I…
Don't you know she's a…
But this how it's always been..
Just a burden of personal demands
Oppressing to repress
Weaving fibers of an impossible feat
For people to just exist.
Don't be too loud, you'll scare people
You shouldn't speak your mind
What if someone judges ME for it
What a poor reflection of ME
Rejection projection
What will people think about ME?
If they hear you
Or comprehend anything you say
Narrowed in from a small peep hole
Careful, not too nude
Clutches them pearly whites
We could never linked up
Because you're a "liability"
To my ego…

Hey, hey look!
Look, this girl obeys
She had molded herself well
Peak performance
Of my ideal expectations
Like plastic
Or a mannequin doll,
Poised for the perfect pussy
Cold fish
Haven't had a hug in weeks
Skin deep,
How do I turn off this doubt?
Why do you have to make this so difficult?!
Why can't you just be normal?
Why can't you just obey?
Behave
Be this
Be less
Be.
Be silent.
Do I look like a receptacle?
Have I become your waitress?
The entitlement
Of expecting someone to change for you
Accommodate so you don't dim their shine
Oppress to fit your box of horrors and deeds
Hold back so that the others can fly high
Can I run away screaming now?
Fleeing from judging jealousy
Ego
We're all smart in our own ways,

My intelligence isn't overwhelming
You might just be intimidated.
Why must I be something else?
Don't you want to know me?
Accept me for who I am
Why have you already decided
I don't fit
Linear thinking in a 5D world
Only angles here
Pay attention!
Too many positions to even contemplate

I'm not going to keep giving access
My time is expensive
No attention to be paid
Registering what I've brought to the table
Subtle and sweetness
Needs a refined and trained eye
They want me!
But at the expense of me
No masters, no gods
My own keeper
Parlay or piss off
Forcing my hand
To become a tolerable presence
Guarantees they silently resent you
In control of the game
A building a pit of rage to consume
Abusing ever part of good
Until it crumbles into yet another failed disaster

Low Point

They saw you at a low
Laughter, pity, ire
Thought they'd see the end
Watching for a grand "finale"
Plotting your demise
Lying in wait to see a failure
But little do know
Realize or understand
Highs and lows
Come naturally to you
Perhaps small minds lack full dimension
The only pleasure derived from others pain
Waiting in the squalor
Matrix of bodies writhing in filth
"Join us…" they moan
Relinquished of standards and drive
Give in to the pressure
Spinning webs of entanglement and lies
"We are the new way forward"
They retort
"It doesn't get better than this"
Echoing long stories past
"Settle for what you have"
Lest you know what is coming next
Babe, they can't even fathom your vision
The way your eyes sparkle
Ideas of grander
No, just a smoking pipe dream
But true innovation
You are GOD among the mortals

Don't forget to rip off your shirt every now and again
Feel the blood pumping through your chest
Down to the loins
A hormonal crux that grabs the neck scruff
Hand delivered will to succeed
Pure heart, the only effective mirror
Covered lips do lie to protect the insecure
Talk of the town to keep a townie
Slice those ties to who was once standing
Replace fables with the rock-hard reality
Known and unknown
You are the master of your own act
Intermission?
Hell, I'm just getting started
Take a seat
Pay my fee
Contact Boundaries
Shut up and listen
Because now,
I'm here to take you on a magical journey
Where the only interludes
Are musically inclined
Pumped with adrenaline
And naked.

Glint

The limerence of
Wish versus
Sobering reality
Is harsh on the senses
Stuck between
Desire and
Tangible
Skimming on skin
Lovely blankets
Comfort places
Things being venusy
Please let me live in
Your world
Take a ride into my psychic side
Walk my lines
The dance
Of tra la la
Beautimus
Ten of libations
Liberating us
From cheek to cheek
I breathe your breath
Chin to cheek
Lips do touch
I can only pretend to
Give you mouth to mouth
If it's not really kissing
But oh how I want to
Bite your lips and show
But I wait patiently
Until the time
Is right

Deftly the White Flag

Defeated
It happens to the best
My heart
Feels so closed
So many misdirects
A lie that resounds
Echos
You want to believe
Someone who acts
Talks
Says trustworthy things
Is real
Why would you lie?
Maybe I'll learn
Really though ask yourself
Why do you need to lie?
What scares you
So much about the truth?
You've hurt me
1,2 punch in the gut
That don't mean you're
Big daddy
Ain't shit
With out consent
Men taking advantage
Of young girls
Power blinds
But who really has
The upper hand?
I don't want
The branch extended
If it is rotten

Flip it on the head
If I am stone
You can't penetrate
My soul
I'd rather choke
Myself
Than stomach
Any more ego
I have no more
To feel
Just walk away
Victory is meaningless
With you
No one wins
Showing only charming
People love the smile
Control freak lives within
Holding me
Withholding what once
Was given
Leaving me begging
For the original
So tricky
Fake
Almost evil
Do I believe intentions
Did you mean to hurt me
Accidentally
Or?
Dare I believe
This person I love
Wants to hurt me
Break down

All what was good
By playing
The victim
Sucker for
A lover who needs love
Sadly then
I'm the dumb dumb
Blamed for falling
Vulnerable
To someone I believed in
Now all I do
Is walk around in suspect
Never fully letting
A guard down
So when you wonder why
She isolates
Seems so miserable
Won't let you close
You leave
It's too hard
Why try with you
Reconfirmed
Her suspicions
You weren't worth it
Talk to your brothers
Call on your friends
Ask of them
Do better
Stop hurting our feminine
Stop allowing
Such poor behavior
Cause you're better than that

CHAPTER 5

Inside Out

My Core

I'm in love with you
I always have been
It just took me a while to get here
You're so hot
Like, I see you and damn
You are perfect just the way you are
You better be careful girl
Ima get you pregnant
But like you're also funny
Quick witted
Like, actually funny
Poised
And you listen
Comprehend
A treasure to be found
I can't believe there is someone like you
Get me, you just know
Feel as if I've known you all my life.
I am so in love
Definitely
Definitely, in love
Withstanding challenges
Doubt
Up against a wall
Defending course
Worth it
Totally worth it
Ima lock you down
Keep this
Forever.

The Mountain

Walking away from bullshit
This week like..
Are you really that lazy?
Are you so focused on your own success..
That you'd sacrifice others
Rude
Who are you miss entitled?
Muttering under your breath at me
Oh, you'd punch me in the face?
Petty violence begets violence
I am a tree
Deep roots and harmonious leaves
But I am also the mountain
I boil deep within
Under the layers of dirt, you threw
I am GAEA
You wanna fuck with me?
I'll blow your ass up
With my hot, hot magma
Get fucked you dumb a$s ho3
Sitting dormant
Lying in wait
Tricky, tricky
Engulfing you with branches until you've disappeared
Sad, pathetic, slovenly
Leech
Not even adding any social grace
Or kindness to any situation
Filthy garbage vomited from your lips
Sour and staining everything around you
I'll let you slip and fall in your own mess

Nothing needed on my part
I am the empress
I am the tree
I am just sitting here waiting and watching
You fall on your own sword
Thinking I was stupid
Projecting your depth of vision onto me
Because all you care about is your selfish ass self.
Poor character is never becoming.
So, I just sit and wait for the wheel to turn
Karma in my favor this time.
Toodles!
See ya never!

Sour Note

The things you say
How they sting
Like searing hot metal
Edged up in the inner thigh
Elongated session on the ribs
Why do you act like that?
Pretend to ignore my feelings
Such a fucking bitch
Do not ever grab me like that again
None of you is, as entitled as you act
Go ahead, project all over me
I suppose I can take it
Pity me for not choking your choices
Yet envy my progress
Elevating into the air
So high
So high
I'm walking on clouds
Activating goddess status
You could have the tools
If you bothered to activate yourself
Not just rely on someone to carry you
Then it's toxic
I can't waste my energy on you
It's like dumping into an endless pit
Needy wanting mouth all the time
Without any respect
Like you don't even give a shit about me
So why should I?

Toxic Femininity

Unkind
Misappropriated
Misdirected words
Cut me off while I'm talking?
Ignore me speaking up
Boom, boom!
Bang, bop!
Here I come to burst your bubble
Excuse you
I see you now
shoving your butthole in my face
Stealing my ideas and practice as your own
Diminishing me in the process
Jealous?
Yeah, dream on
You can never be me
But you get to be you
And I guess that's ok?
Focused on my goals
Glow up to show up
I didn't waste time on frivolous things
Direct and focused
To the point
Sharpened up and poof
Here is my sword
Swallow it or face worse
Sparkle, sparkle, bitch
And yes, I am looking at myself in the mirror
You know, while you go on about yourself
Not that you're not interesting
Train wrecks are hard to look away from.

Oh, was that too harsh?
I'm sorry, would you like to fix your life?
Show me the money
You know,
So, I can eat!
Intellectual property ain't free
Keep chugging though
Choo, choo motherfucker
Here comes the train
Sooo judgmental
I see your eyes dart
Telling a story
More high ground
The "alpha" female
False confidence of fitting into an expectation
Undercutting and stealing to hold down others
Careful you don't fall off your pedestal, dear
Lest you might be down here with us mortals
Such flawed creatures
Hope you don't scare easy
I drag you along out of willingness
The kindness of friendship
No woman left behind
Upon arrival,
You're there: squawking a distraction
Boasting about how you made it
No acknowledgement of my hard work
I can't speak to you in truths?
No nursemaid or bitch here
Rejected from my life
Unworthy of my nurturing

Sit your bony ass down and take notes
Credit where it's due
Without me
You'd still be fucking different cocks every night
Choking on dick as not to think
Bemoaning "all men are trash!"
You are what you eat sweetie
Or hidden under your comforter
In tears slobbering
"Why am I stuck?"
Probably because you lack internal compassion for anyone including yourself.
Playing victim and victor in one sentence
Let's not split hairs
Who is the deity here?
Selfless ain't real
More like self-involved
Self-aggrandizing
Input needs a source
Here's looking at me kid.
Good luck to you though,
You're going to need it

Body Talk

Am I svelte enough for you?
How you like me with curves?
Or do I reflect back
A version of self-love that you hate.
Yes, I know I am beautiful
I make a deafening sound when I walk
But not from bent floorboards
Not the sound of my clapping thighs
My body is none of your business
Talk about its shape
Solid food in the mouth
Skimpy stretched things over sturdy hips
My autotomy is that I make the final call
So please
Step off bitch
I don't care for your side coaching
For you are slave to outside sources
The approval of others
Monkey mind
Spinning hamster on the wheel
Gotta look better
Must improve
Or I will lose my sculpted power
That given to me by those
Who wish to knock me off
That pedestal we all sit on
Needing approval that we
In fact are attractive
Possibly worthy
For someone who is not equip to handle
All of these goodies
So put your milk shake to the streets
Put out a milky streak
I live freely
Only here to please myself

Cracked Reality

Every moment lead us back here
Where time has no direction or consistency
Unlocking a divine pathway
Slowly uncovering a passionate mystery
Glimpses of the golden desire

I saw it then, misty and brief
Unsure of what truly was
Following symbols and signs
Neon or more subtle

I've apologized enough for what wasn't my fault
However, I did lie
I wrote a letter but omitted the most important detail
I could have written you a whole book of my love

But would you have accepted it, me?
Afraid of your life
What was out of my control
Not considering the complexity of mine

Maybe we were both lying
Ignoring the red-hot elephant in the room
Because it was easier than opening up
A false sense of security holding on to a secret

Fear, with liquor on her lips
Eyes, that cannot lie
I stared, looking for meaning in yours
Yearning to ask the questions I couldn't verbalize
Not trusting to be answered truthfully

A sweet and painful layover of star-crossed paths
Casual conversation
Straining with the depth of underpinnings
Just a dash of psychological disposition

As if forces beyond the earthly plane
Had begun to spin a weaving web of desire
So intense, a fire raging untended
Unstoppable, cleansing all in its path

As I laid freshly inked, in your bed
Not touching, but in a room as hot as the tension between us
Invisible barrier screaming caution between
Tossing and turning as if to shake it off
I wondered if you could feel the energy too

I couldn't,
I just couldn't tell you.
What if you laughed, were silent or even worse?
Direct eye contact in that brief moment
Between chaos and quiet
And said, "come on Nicole, what did you expect?"

Little to no recognition
Unready, I realized
Too lost in your own tasty ego sauce
Drowning in bad influences with no filter

You were going to have to break your own heart
Using that girl as a tool for your own destruction
I, being the bystander who couldn't look away
Reluctantly leaned in to hug you
The only time our two bodies had touched
Not wanting to pull away
Yet fearing what kind of portal I was being pulled into

I felt so helpless
Swallowing my pride and selfish thoughts
Sticking in my throat creating the first barrier
It was never really about who won or lost
Each to suffer the same uneasy fate
Anger wasn't my friend here
Silence was both my friend and enemy
Taunting my willpower in each empty moment
I had to learn how to make peace with both

The contract demands both recognize
Running away was the option I took
But you opened the door
Lodged a wedge nice and tight between the ground
Left open, only watching from a far
Never crossing any inappropriate walls
I wouldn't let you
Your pride toed the line hard
My mind and heart needed to get right
For when fate decided to steer this train back
I would be ready this time

The Consistent Question

What is love?
Is there even a consensus of what is all contains?
Styles and types
Levels of connection
What comprises to become deeper
More intensely held in our hearts
Patience for someone who isn't quite on the same page?
Definitely not an ultimatum or forcing of certain behaviors.
Deeper understanding for something done a different way?
Embracing a success or win even if it doesn't belong to you?
It's messy for sure
Confusing and rewarding at the same time
Shifting and changing your prospective on what is important.
Flawed in many aspects
Defined, undefined and living in a headspace unspoken
Doesn't live up to magazine covers, tabloids or gossip
It's real; real emotion, gritty and uncomfortable
A deeper knowing or acknowledgment of what really is there for you
Boundaries or unbounded in between those who agreed
There is vulnerability and seeing things that was once judged before
Watching someone make a mistake
Knowing the pain, it will cause and committing to help pick up the pieces after
Snotted up nose and tears wiped away
A warm embrace with our expectations
Complete lack of control over another
It's trust that what is put in, will come out
Not here to win an award or brag to a friend
No empty promises or grandiose gestures of appeasement
Chaos and harmony wrapped together

Twisting and flowing further into the unknown
A promise to be authentic in all you do
A hope for a better future outcome
Yet sitting with what is in the here and now
No schematic or blueprint
Just some blind faith and a bit of magik
Starting each day as a brand new shiny open path.

Taking Names

Those whose names we know
You have been here for us all along
But who really are you?
That is for only you to know
For when you lived with us
They didn't notice you
Did you breathe the air I did?
Laughed right along beside me?
Languished in the waves?
Or have you shifted me
Into next of kind consciousness
Because I felt safe
Because I felt whole
You smiled at me
And I knew you
At least I thought
I was confident and self-assured
Your eyes holding me in grace
I couldn't hold you
Not in my arms
But in the idea that moments are temporary
That here in the time
Mere seconds
Shared between us
That time existed much deeper
Extended paces of boundaryless light
This is where I could breathe again

Again

If I ever see you again,
I will show you
How I feel.
Live in wait
Those stolen moments,
Wherein I peeked
Within.
Naked.
So naked.
Before your body
souls to be seen,
Such honesty
Seeped in.
This way and that.
All I wanted to see
Was your success,
Your happiness.
Words sometimes
Not nearly enough,
For such passion
Raging inside.
I want your expression,
Coat me with some fine flannel.
Laughter ringing in the wind.
Staring at me,
Speaking so subtle
But soft.
Whispered the truth

With your eyes.
Laying the path
Brick by brick,
In my hearts path,
To ultimate dominion.
King of kings
Don't you hide who you are.
Tell me,
How much you desire
Such royalty
To hold your heart.
Through this mysterious,
Wildly ambiguous
Destiny of life.
No distance,
Is truly between us.
When once we agreed,
To find one another
Over and over
Again

CHAPTER 6

Realizations

Pattern Breaker

Settled for what I got
Always just a friend never the main
They could confide with my gentle mind
Never judgmental one to find
But I'd hide how I really felt
Never stand out lest I expose myself
If I loved him, he'd never know
Just blow me off and take her to the show
My worth was defined so low
By the dregs sniffed out my insecurity
Because I didn't love myself
That course was never taught in school
Straight A's to learn the world
But little did I know myself
The virginal slut they pointed fingers
No energy to defend myself
The depth I hid behind fake walls
Because no one could handle the intensity
So even in relationships I was never seen
But maybe if I lived up to what they pretended
The ideas that were popular enough
Someone might recognize me
But you didn't
And I did
Rejection stings worse from you
Then ever by jerk off's with their rocks off
That's why no one could compare
But if I give you such a pass
Instead of taking it slow we crash
Even after I strip down

Naked under all these layers
Broke through the patterns I relied upon
Rejected what was no longer good for me
We'd still be on repeat
Still remind you of a girl
Like a brand-new child
Take those baby steps
Not take it so easily in depth
Use one another like a drug just stop hurt
Encourage the rise from fall point
But do it separate instead of holding on
This time I'm not trying to fuck it up
I wanna do right by us
Because if we can figure out
Decode communication
I think this could go the distance
No matter how many stabs we've taken
How far we had fallen on our knees
The differences we both know
How to get back up

Ghosting

Screaming
In my head
In my heart
If only I could
If only
I try so hard
To believe
I want to believe
I want you to believe in my:
Brave faces
Hold places
Lifting the value to what is accepted
Yet,
Yet.
Why can you not see?
What is blinding you?
Wipe your eyes dear
The tears are all dried now
The pain is not here anymore
Here I am
Just a girl
Standing here in front of you
I hold in my hand a shiny object
That which you can see
A reflection clear as day
But you refuse to look.
Why?
Are you afraid of what you might see
The dark storms?
Monsters reaching twisted fingers
Over broad and proud shoulders
What do you expect my dear?

The anger you hold within
The failure of past, present to be future tense?
Are you tense in those shoulders?
Carrying that unnecessary load?
I know you're use to holding on
It makes you feel safe.
Or perceive what is safe
Because it is familiar
Tigers are familiar with snakes
But a poison fang will take your life
Do not let it take your life from you
You have not lived this long
Achieved so much
So that one pointy prick
One bitch knocks you down
You are a fighter
Maybe there be fear in your heart
But not in your eyes
And fear is just lack of faith in the unknown
But you have done many things
Unknowing of what will come
I ask this of you
With tears in my eyes
That's stream down my face
Leaving me cleansed
Let it go
Do not hold the anger the shame
The pain is no longer necessary
For the lesson has come to pass
And you can heal
Let yourself
Let go
You can see
Me

Love Drunk

I created a fantasy of you
I wanted it to be true
Drowning in the mystery
Covered my eyes
Swallowed the medicine
Believing obvious tall tales
I saw what I wanted
I wanted it to be you
But what now?
The cold hard reality of facades
Draped curtains
Bleeding into the water
I can still smell you
Lime, coconut and lies
How sweet the salty rim is
Take a sip of your tenuous tequila nightmares
Golden sunrise dreams
Maddening visions in my brain
Reaching for desires, just out of grasp
I wail
Feelings, all the feelings leak out of sad sockets
I want the reality this time
But a stable rock formed over time
I want to believe in what you say
Know that tomorrow it will stay the same
Ruts to become reliable
Give me your predictable, tradition
I can have faith in that
I'll be there for this type of love

Sober reality
No longer hazy hangovers, no stan changing motives
I trust in this fall
I might land on my ass time to time
But there is a seat reserved at this table
Every day, same time
Same face.
No bull, just the cud.
Can you feel me?
I know what I want now, do you?

Sealed with a Blade

Here
I brought you something
Gift wrapped and tied up with a bow
I wanted to make it perfect for you
Couldn't say no
Here
Put your ear to the box and you might hear it
Thump
So mysterious wrapped up in so many layers
But just one sound gives it away
It's my heart
I gave you it
I decided it was only for you
Cut open my chest cavity
Maneuvered the scalpel
Severed the main artery
I thought I knew what I was doing
Blinded by the gift
My heart is only for you
No one else should have it
A weak smile
As my face turns paler
Grasping
Gasping for breath as my handshakes
I hold out the box
With my still beating heart
So still, it beats for you
You look down with disgust
Maybe some pity

And sneer
I'm choking now
Still holding the box as I die
Ignoring my symptoms, you get up and leave
My heart
Oh, my heart!
You told me someone broke yours
So, I tried to replace it
And you broke mine instead
You broke my FUCKING heart
But you're still alive
I don't know if I am

Sobering Up

How much can the human heart bear
The weight of a thousand shameful slights
Slander of the greatest kinds vast and deep
Destructive forces of those who snide upfront
Grotesque forms of human configuration
Linking one to another for purposes of pain
Sturdy structures found flimsy under pressure
Except that furious axe swings are applied
Repeatedly to dismantle the mountain of good will
She kneels in mud and putrid thoughts
Knowing the disgusting and vile that had been abandoned upon her
Shoulders fatigued no longer holding the story
Not only so he won't repeat it, as she just cannot bear it anymore
Gasping for last breaths
Crushed by the weight of a crush that only pierces and punctures
Joy so far from what seems to be the full reality
Yet longing for the lover's touch
Will he
Would he
Reach out a kind hand
Make a move and act upon empty promises?
Lift the mess dumped, duped upon a kind heart
Toxic they say
But aren't we all in our own mess
Some just accept more than can be taken
Being toxic within itself
Can she forgive
Herself
For abandoning her own needs
So willingly to aid a love
A love so hopeful
Perhaps delusional

That hope may destruct her
Unless her mass of inner strength
Built a silent reserve
From all the previous grievances
Pure and utter demolished social reputations
Brought upon fake friends, love interests
She had been here before
Never though, from him
He was supposed to be infallible
Yet, a human being with flaws just the same
Forgiveness is a virtue not to be sniffed at
Because it is the very thing that will save us
From ourselves
When looking in the mirror, the flaws infuriating us
Are just those reflected by whom we choose
Did I fear being deconstructed by you?
That I couldn't be honest enough with my love for you?
Because I just wanted you to choose me to be that mirror
Don't be afraid of that, I will not die or crack
Maybe you thought I would shatter your masked perception
Premature face lifting, soul splitting
But I think you're ready now for me
Please don't run again
I need someone to help lift the collapse of chaos upon me
I don't want to do it alone again
You shouldn't have to do it alone again.

Done and Dusted

The cruelest goodbye
Picking the needles out of my back
As I stare off into the distance
Glazed eyes
Thinking of anything but the pain
Worst is I did it to myself
As if there was any alternative
Can't change the past
Tried to influence the future
But now
I am the present
Only peace I'll know
Is to be right here
Letting go of waiting
Grasping carefully to the needles
As not to let draw blood
Maybe I need to bleed just a little
Mindful of where pain lies
Could stop at any time
But I want to hold on
Delay myself, suspended for unknown
Time isn't real anyways
Even when it's wrong, it's still a gift
Paralyzed searching for land mines
Secret traps overlooked
As if there was anything I could do
Change a stubborn mind
But maybe, just perhaps
That space and time was given
Not as a punishment
Through I'd fitfully seen it as so

That goodbye kiss as I mournfully remembered
Fantasizing of my lips meeting yours finally
First and seemingly last
Thought to be kicked out of your vision
It was just the prelude to evolution
The invitation to a new portal
A rope so invisible had already existed between
In my own way that I couldn't see
My scaled mountains
I was the prototype
Showing you how it could be done
Instead of pushing or pulling
There was just enough length
As a guided tour
So, you could admire my ass
As I lead the way

Divine Surrender

If I can't have you
Timelines won't match up
Cards read a no
You choose not to take that path
There is nothing I can do
It'll hurt like hell
Oh, the shreds of my heart
Flooded basement of tears
As I float in my misery
I'll wish well to you
Bless the way forward
Knowing it's the gods will
Universal judgement
Acceptance is the key to my exit
Escaping rejection
To protect me from more pain
What is meant for me is yet to be
Divinely orchestrated operetta
Singing my song
Telling life with the words written
Henceforth I surrender to what is
Can no longer carry this anger
What good would it do for me
Even if I got what I wanted by force
It wouldn't mean much
Voluntary selection of desire
So much more satisfying
Tied deeply into your essence
Borderline obsessed
But is it right for me

Never thought I could release your ghost
You'll always be my friend
Wanted the best of you
For you
All of my love to you
Maybe someday I can have it in return
But for now
I surrender
To what is

CHAPTER 7

Secrets Grow in the Dark

Hidden Realms

Secret indulgences kept their claws in me
Although technically unavailable
Still a sneaky link
Chained, bound, gagged and stuck
A pretty little pet
Had me right where you wanted
Always a safe bet behind scenes
Technology leading to effortless spying
Even if the consciousness wasn't always so
People are aware of what they do
Public, private which face is showing?
Even if you don't get what you need at home
There for a pick me up in sickness
Where there is lack in known spaces
Call her a friend to satisfy connection
But the sting of abandonment
Speaks volumes overhead
Satisfying how little someone asked for
Or was willing to accept
Yet knocked off the perch
Fiending for that ego hit
The price got higher
Worth: what does it mean to you?
Accepting bare minimum at lowest cost of self
I never asked, how dare the shift change?
Too much emotional labor breaking the bottom line
But I still need it
Don't know how to produce, yet the well has dried
Replacements ever so cheap and break almost instantaneously
Nothing can replace the original

Satisfying that itch only becomes a greater obsession
Gratification needs highly specific
Even with all the ingredients
Without her that trigger won't hit
Functioning addict on the outside
Seemingly satisfied in life path choices
Yet once taste hits the tongue
Full of flavor and hidden notes
Ranges that have never been hit before
Highest highs counterbalancing
Natural routine lows, adjusted for functioning
You can never go back, and you can never forget.

Maiden Voyage

To the sea and the tides
Sand and fresh salty air
Open waters release cumbersome binds
Sail away on floating barges
The sunset envelopes
Swallowing like a portal
Escaped the matted forest
Mess of vines and pitfalls
The snakes have stopped biting
Ragged branches no longer scratching
Humidity breeding more mosquitos fading
Deep breath in
Fully extended lungs and belly
No more restriction
Sun rays sparkle off of dazzling clear blue
Washing face in the waves
I am clean again
Whole again
Seeing a reflection mirrored back
Perceptive as the day
Not shade from trees standing long with judgement
Pretending to be secure shelter
But filled with more venom than peace
Never again he cried wading into low tide
Serene calm water folds gently into him
Cleansing the rest of his body and soul
Not taking any last look at the jungle
Where his captivity harangued his mentality
Insanity whispered from each vicious leaf
Predators waited water tongues for his demise

He fully immersed himself in safety of the open water
After what seemed to be a face swimming by
Scales of blue with one long fanatical fin
His head bobbed up in surprise that he might not be alone
A miracle? A mirage?
Or a mind tricked hallucination?
As his eyes focused a vessel suddenly in view
He gasped
Waving his arms, he made a commotion
"Help! Help! I am here, please take me with you!"
His cries, not in vain
Heralded a floatation tied with steady rope
Docked to the ship
A sigh of relief escaped his lips
Hand extended, reached his grip
Met a gaze familiar, yet mysterious
Those eyes.
She smiled at him with an echo of home and said
"Welcome aboard, where would you like to go?"

Switching Gears

The art of letting go
Detaching oneself from just a complex discord
Unpacking, unearthing, demolishing
The old roots
Dead, decayed and no longer fruitful
Useless, unstable, in the way
But why is it so difficult to complete the task
A memory of what could have been
The peach tree to bring summer fruit
Rotten pits in sour stomachs
Vomiting up dreams of better days
Fuck those low hanging fruits
Who decided to keep germinating them?
Disguised as sweet succulents
But tasteless in the core
Peering across to the abandoned lot
Long forgotten as it was by the city and all others
Unappealing and mistaken for barren
Rough ground of rocks, concrete, rubbish
Focused on your seedless, tasteless Prunus
Wishing and willing it to become the picture perfection
Unaware of the team of volunteers
Slowly, humbly cleaning up next door
Unearthing raw soil
Fragrant dirt rife with nutrients for growth
A garden of wildflowers amongst sweet grass
Redwood tree shooting its baby sprouts
Soon to bring clean air and shade
Tended to, cared for by those who saw potential
A small patch of love shining brightly
Beauty from a dumping ground of careless losers
A slice of heaven, waiting to be snatched up

Playful Park for those in need
Now looking back at the barren garden
Garden of empty memories
The gardener, covered in dust and hanging his head
Gutted, psychological wasteland
Drained of nurturing, face value and cash
Staked a for sale sign in front of the empty house
Relenting that growth will never happen here
Crossing the street, he falls short of the serene lot
Tears fall hitting the pavement
A crack beneath his feet
A small flower poking its face through
Seeming to sprout out of nowhere
Confused he stood in bewilderment
Could this pain water future roots
Lost in thoughts of better days
A large monster truck's wheels squealed
Nearly a terrible collision
Life almost over in one fatal swoop
Carelessly unaware of what could be
Focused on lost opportunities
Dead leaves
Shitty dead blooms
Falling face first into the soft patch of grass
Sweet wafts of tender scent kiss his nose
Shaded from harsh elements
A haze of exhaustion and serenity fell over
Eyes grew heavy and lids slid down
Dreamy visions appearing in vortexes subconsciously
Fast asleep in the space, once deemed uninhabitable
Soundly he slept, dreaming big dreams of tomorrow

Becoming the Master

Are you afraid you're not enough?
From the times before when it failed
They abandoned ship
Chemistry fizzled quickly
Nothing was ever good enough
Tricked you into being an option
Do you think you know what love is?
A substitute never could quench
However here it is.
Different
Rather, teaching you
Cannot be controlled
Forced or planned
It's a feeling
No matter how much you deny
Ignore your intuition
Indulge in the moment to drown yourself
Keep going
Don't stay in hell
Why would you needlessly suffer
For someone who deceived you?
I realize now
If you've never had a love like this
Imagining it to be unreal
The struggle to believe
You'd choose "good enough"
Unless the universe made it so uncomfortable
Had to move
Painful as it is
Difficult for those in their ruts
Change has a purpose

Wandered too far off path?
Drowned out internal navigation
With pills, potions
Whisky full stop
Damn near determined to kill yourself
Dying will to believe
You let her deny yourself
Wormed claws into your brain
Viper with golden dreams in the eyes
A meal ticket of a human
Narcissists never see the humanity in their victims
Just a means to an end
Nothing will satisfy their thirst for soul sucking
As they lack anything of substance
Your virtue is tasty
Sweetness stacked tall
A lover through and through
Ambition and brains
Rejection is protection mi amore
Reroute the navigation back to success
Played a good hand
However, true love trumps the devil in a smock
Good sex is just the chain to keep the hungry bound
One day the mask slips
Insipid personality exposed
Don't be embarrassed
Someone's inability to love you
Is only a reflection of the deep wounds they carry
Don't fix what you didn't break
The father you seek lives within you

I feel the heart in you
Reflect it back
Forgiveness of the kindhearted
Give yourself a chance to prove
That the cycle can be broken
A family trauma infects us until we say no more
Finding who you are
Comes in the quiet moments
Not where the spotlight shines
But you can still be that star
You are one in my eyes
One day your mirror will be cleaned
Tears dried
Pride mended
You will finally see the truth
Whole reflection of your inner self
A true champion
Master of head and heart

Imposter Syndrome

Maybe it just isn't
Maybe I was right to walk out
Exist in a space you may never
It seems uneven at first glance
Embracing the life
They all dream of
Someone who enjoys solitude
Ignored, forgotten by all
No room or reason to perform
Even though I'm a natural
I'd rather disappear
Be alone with my thoughts and feelings
Few and none to vocalize
At least not on the surface where you reside
Mocked for not going along with the tide
Ostracized from the groups
Loaner
Insulted by those who have no leg to stand alone
My strength self-contained
The grace of knowing that nothing is ever what it seems
An asshole isn't always that
But someone who repels and has been rejected
By those who don't bother to understand
A smiling face isn't always kind
A beauty isn't always natural
Yet we are expected or find that is reinforced
Role models of epic proportions
Live in misery, charging the utmost for their peep show
Keeping up with what?
At least I am free
I live my life by the rules I agree upon

Displease those who lack imaginative expansion
I know what people think
I can hear them
Silently or blaringly in my head
The judgement of all that is
Due to the lack of self-love
Projection of inner failings
Seeing someone secure and wishing to tear it down
I see you, living in fear
That someone might actually see you
What they would do with that
Rather than embrace the weird
Individualistic play and spirit of life
You'd rather fit in
Be the hero
Enjoy the false admirations
Fall in lust with the same mistake over and over
Be predictable as the bull out to pasture
Living a lie to comfort your wounded heart
Suffering the emptiness, it brings
A shallow meaningless existence
Starring through the glass
At those freely playing in the wind
Watching my every move
Yet lacking the courage to join me.

Difficult Maps

I wonder
How did it end up to be
Wrong choice
Trounced by a bitch on wheels
Ate up her lies
Hook, line and sinker
Mourning in the madness
In love with a cheater
Thought the one, a decal
Tinsel on a trash can
Dragged to hell and back
Each dart of the tongue a dagger
Besmirched reputation for glory
Gory gold digging with no mercy
Gaslighter of the century
Showing just a fraction of the toxicity
Carried on cycle to cycle
Embraced what you thought you wanted
Familiar far too comfortable
Kicking and screaming shoved from the nest
Hardly could look at something new
Walking around like a blind man
Feeling up your hands
On any chest that thrusts forward
You were lost when I met you
Seem to be still wandering
I thought you'd finally see me
By now the recollection would tip off
Because I'm a wanderer too
Maybe you and I had our chance

I can't make you love me
It's not fair to still chase you
Put my heart on the line
Time and again
When you've only teased
Are you too proud to admit how you really feel?
How many times you want to fall
Before accepting life's gift
What you asked for
Maybe in a different package
But perhaps
Those superficial differences
Aren't what make it love
Perhaps you've got some flaws as well
Things that would turn some sour
True love not in spite of
Embracing the whole of you
Not to change core values
Cheering the growth that comes
From two people finally giving up the fight
Friends become lovers
Lovers find the quiet space
Calm brings peace.

Navigating by the Stars

Believe it
As the sun comes up everyday
Rain falls saturating the soil
Green shoots grow
Sprout vividly colored flowers
You too shall become whole again
Though the days continue
Life seemingly unceasing
Some days there is an end
Misfortune and unanswered questions
Prayers that seem to go unheard
How do you believe it
The faith in happiness
That good things and people will be
Each time you climb a step
There are hidden enemies and push back
Sabotage and self-sabotage

A fake out waiting to utilize your reaction
Hiding in the shadows
Anxiety makes itself known
Who or what can be trusted
How do I have faith in such unknowns
The signs and symbols flare
Yet go unnoticed to those distracted
Do I really know?
Or is it wishful thinking?
Wanting to believe so intensely
I've convinced myself
Of a lie
Or was it?

Having faith in someone seems near impossible
With flaws and failures
When they don't even believe themselves
You can lie to everyone else
But you cannot lie to yourself
Or me.
It's called "the game"
Moving parts
Hidden motives
Action to reaction
Vigilant to behavior
Noticing the minute details of eye movements
To win the game you best the person
Make them fall for a lie

What if
Just what if
Actually winning
Meant that you change the game?
Do all the wrong things
According to acquaintances
Look like a fool to your peers
Save no face
But climb deep within the heart space
Authentic acts of pure loves service
An unconditional belief
That what you put out
Will come back in multitudes
Break the mold

What if doing the very thing
Warned against by those who thought they knew
Was the key
To unlock your own heart
Unfurling a constantly changing map
Realistically to life's realities
Each step revealed along the way
As long as attention was paid
Careful dedication to the path ahead
No ruts or stagnant beliefs could stay
Getting what you want requires uncertainty
At times there will be nothing to reassure you
That is when there is faith

Trusting your own heart
To lead you
Shed all expectations
Outside opinions become muted
In the silence
Only then can you hear the beating of two hearts
Briefly,
Until the sound of life come screaming back
Under the influence again
Tapped into superficial conditions
Grounding effects
Heart beating in the chest remind us
Everyday
To have faith.

Releasing the Anchor

If it goes let it go
If it clings walk away
The action of energy
Should never be forced
You are not too much
What you bring to the table
Is to be celebrated
Cherished
Revered
Free to pursue life on your terms
You owe nothing to no one
Even when you're alone with wins
Or alone in misery
You are worthy of love
The most potent love
Echoing from the deepest corners
Vibrating underneath the lowest frustrations
Pain can be so loud
Used as tools by the vitriol of secret enemies
It's easy to hurt a vulnerable person
Not something to take pride in
We hurt ourselves everyday
Unclear of what is acceptable
Afraid to stand alone
But solitude becomes addictive
The amount of control
The peace
Observing the massive change
Comfortably in discomfort
Becoming brand new

Maybe unfamiliar to past parts
Grieving the idea of self
That person couldn't make it this far
Something had to give
To get what you really want
A sacrifice of all that didn't pass
The strength to level up
To move forward and forgive the past
Is honorable
It takes time and should come naturally
Yet, don't resist it
For it is the greatest gift you get
A new life
A chance to become better than before
Change is inevitable
Ride the waves
Be open to receive
Step up into the life you've wanted
Fear is just the coat challenge wears
Nothing good will be easy
Don't stop before the finish

New Horizons

I thought I'd die without you
Maybe I am dramatic
So what
Nothing spices up life
Like a little emotion
Deity knows there isn't enough
Empty vessel robotics
Mechanically repeating day to day
But my dear
What did you expect
Leaving me in the lurch
Only to watch longingly from afar
I'd rather be eccentric
An anomaly
A spectacle entertaining

Darling, I did die
I changed
Became a person who was self-reliant
Attitude changed
Not controlled by sexual desires
Unswayed by public opinion
Unbiased of identity's that do not match
Quit hangers on
Deleted my history of pleasing
Anyone else but me
Much to the chagrin of those
Who needed my action
Feeling superior

Profited
Railroading
Destroyed fully
Slowly chip away at my self esteem
Knowing my intimate secrets
Played to be trusted
Yet quietly hated
As I was offering my neck for life blood
Vampires.
Daemons
In human form
Only to denigrate me in the under breath

But is it dramatic to respond to disrespect
Holding the world on your shoulders
Details will be missed
Did you miss me?
Or just decide I wasn't good enough
For the illusions you held for your life
Let it crash all down
Holding on only makes it worse
Self-deception is the most dangerous beast
Tangled between confidence and ego
Repressed anger growls
Toppling over the easily offended
Words cannot be violent
Distain is not a weapon that kills
Tone is not a gun to your temple demanding
Fuck you, shouldn't be a curse

Nothing about me is the same
The new me is aware
Which is close to the physical death
As memories resurface in grudges
Only those who remain unchanged
Would believe that no one else grows
I'd rather have all the past versions to throw flowers
Then unrealistic beliefs recounted
The benefit of not being acknowledged
Is that it is so easy to deny the good
Knowing of victimization
Though not of victim mentality
There is always a choice
Freedom
Escape

Promising Timelines

I am free
Removed myself from the clutches
Stepped back
Saw what I needed to see
Faded heart strings
I believed kept me bound and gagged
I am free
Closed my eyes
Became dust in the breeze
You could have untied me anytime
There was a chance to be real
Only manipulations
So much left to be unknotted
Chain bound to your ankles
You carry a heavy burden of your own making
I am not the one to carry it
Wind cannot carry the weight of a thousand slights
No one should
Yet some are willing to receive what isn't theirs
I am free
Detangled from the web of limiting beliefs
Where flood of emotions had been stopped up
How can hope spring from dried bush?
Fighting the good fight
Only with a participant
Crumbs do not proceed dinner
I wrote and wrote
All that could be bothered from my heart
The scope of where it applied was limited
Tried to show you a hard-earned lesson

Short cut
Some truth and clarity
But you chose to stay blind.
I am free
The chord is severed
Pulled out from both ends
It needn't be a bother anymore
No high expectations of quality living
Sight through dark times
You clearly already know
Who am I to teach you?
You are free to continue the cycles
But I am free of you
The grieving is over.

Secret Islands

In the quiet she roams
Peaceful in a tranquil space
The gleam, it pours down
lighting up her body
Fresh grapes glowing
The smell, intoxicating
Anything seems possible
Lying in wait to come into being
Vibrancy off of the molecules
All living beings, alert and instinctual
Gently buzzing in the air space
The hum of natural life going about
There is a harmony within
As so above and below
Beauty mixes and meshes
Fertile ground for future expansion
Dreams are just the beginning
A new chapter
The next season
Where it all happens
Believe in all notions
Big or small
An electrical current to nurture

Balanced with a hard line
Protect and deliver
Standing tall and unwavering
An external force
The commanding, calm, cool and collected
Aware of all that surrounds

Merging the two paradigms may pose a challenge
Yet the interlocking pieces
Magnetically drawn
Could not be stopped
Raging impulse
Paired with a poised reception
 How could the invitation be resisted?
In uncharted territories and unfamiliar terrain
Proceed with caution
For navigation may need translation
Plunged deep into the impacted waters of desire
A bit cooler, sound of the pulse getting louder
What do you want?"
"How hard are you willing to go?"
"What is stopping you?"
In the silence drowned state
Muted reality
The dire need is screaming
Gasping for air
Assess
Act thoughtfully
Prosper.

Masters to Lead

Follow the leader
Me, myself and I
The strength of 10,000
In one righteous soul
God of war's fire runs through
True redemption awaits
The light at the end of a long burdensome tunnel
I am the king, ruler of all four elements
Bravery doesn't begin to define me
Growing pains made me who I am today
Delivered from evil forces sent against me
Accountable for all things
I've carried the responsibility before
I know what it feels like
Four study walls
Stable hand
Unflinching mind
I am ready
I am free
Make the choices needed
For my sanity
Sanctity
Dreams remind me of what was overlooked
I see
I hear
I know all things
Needed on my quest
To possessing the faith
Of which I am and always belonged to
The purity of heart, body and soul
I will return to the motherland
Where love resides
I'm coming home

Dance Gods

The love of my life
You'll always be
Even if I never see you again
At times I've retired myself to
Believing it was a fever dream
I was only granted a taste
So exquisite I had to remember ever second
The way your lips tasted
That tongue tried to wear me from the inside out
No matter where I'm at I can transport back to you
It's a gift and curse
The quiet part I'm not supposed to say
I wonder if you feel it too
Lie away at night
Next to whomever fills the space
Feel my hands touch your face
In the loving way I show you
That yours is the only one that made me feel this
Do you feel my heart choke when I can't breathe
Little plopping tears that roll down my chin?
My head rest upon your chest
Maybe if I sigh hard enough, I can take your breath away
The last bit of connection to you
I may ever feel again
It's hard to let you go
None of it even makes rational sense
Yet here I am struggling to comprehend it
I have to know
Throat tightened with sobs
A routine is hard to break

Stead fasting heart will chug along to the very end
The end of me is the end of you
In this world of cynics
Critics and assholes
Who refuse to be loved
I want to defy their gaffs and malcontent
You can be love as deep as you want to
Secretly we all want it.
Love me as deeply as you need
Drowned in my own fantasy
Tap it to the main vein
Get me high and I'll melt into you
Love is the worst drug
Yet the best fleeting moments
It can become everything and nothing
All you have to do is believe in it
Close my eyes and sleep a thousand years
Meet me there
I'll be dancing just for you.

CHAPTER 8

End of the Beginning

Bye, Bye Bully

Talk talk talk
Bully walk walk walk
Let your lies fly
No one is as dumb as you
Squawk squawk squawk
Not going to balk
See through your games
Child's play you psycho
Powers die spinning your shitty web
Brittle as old leather
Caught in a position refusing to change
Rather bleed a captive dry
Insecurity has you lacking confidential confidence
Failure is imminent to the fool
Who refuses to see their shortcomings
Karma karmic
Here for a season
Reason to breathe your toxic breath
Need contrast to see the light
Threats are empty
Bleach your mouth
When I pop your tongue
Rip it out and play it like a song
Words are one flavor
But intentions aimed to kill
Are not welcome in this chapter
Remove the blade you use to thrill
Falling on others' swords in secret
I'll take mine back
Had enough of your uneven slack
Such weakness is so clear to me

Your "love" is just a learning lesson
To show what isn't meant to be
Bite me?
I'll bite back, harder
Rip you to pieces
The master and misses
Fully grown and whole
I don't fuck with fragments
Play the victim one more time
Just parent lessons
Dealing with an uncontrollable terror
Dis season we're serving well fed
Pear shaped don't lose their squeezability
Beware of the edges
Diamonds will cut you up
Handle with caution
I ain't your friend
You a nightmare from chaos
Beep beep
Time to wake up
Sweating and tired
Tied up in your own mess
Of all the bullshit you slinging
Begone raggedy bitch
I banish you

Totaled

When I crash to the ground
An unyielding fiery blaze blown apart
No one came to look for survivors
Devastation seems so great
A total bodyslam of fuckboi one after another
Pretending to care with false promises and gestures
Laying in our beds waiting for "something better"
Words not matching actions
Toxic polyamory just for the show
Painted so great to fall so low
All with a self deprecating critical eye
I too have been victimized by a covert Narcissist
Hate all you want, you know it's true you messy chaotic bastards
But this story isn't about you.
It's about how I rise
How I was ignored, oh the angry voices
Of those who didn't like my dissent
That thrived when I was silently supporting
But would not raise a finger for me
Who needed me but didn't acknowledge my needs
To this point I say go fuck yourself
Because being a bigger person at this point
Does not mean I will continue to be silent
I am strong and flexible
I am a survivor
I cut off all the deadweight
Maybe a metaphorical limb
I was left to die
By those in a community only out for themselves
Bye boys who cosplay as men
Be alcoholics and drug addicts

So dissolved in their own mess
There was no care about mine
This is the new day
Where rapists will burn
False friends will fall on their faces
Toxic feminine predators get their comeuppance
Creeps in the DM's get a loud resounding "Hell no!
The power structure changes
No longer will communities be centered
Around men using everyone for their game
We are not players
We are warriors
You Christopher Columbus ass bastards
You discovered nothing
Cycle breakers
Leaders, mothers, helpers.
Bow to us now, we are the captain.

Dismissed

Oh sir, excuse me sir
I believed you dropped your decorum
Yeah so, thanks but no.
Too many communication issues
Not a single desire to play you therapist.
Very little attraction
Keep on keeping on whatever little dying connection
Let me pick up your jaw off the floor
Along side your misrepresented expectations
No one has probably said this to you
You ain't a bad dude,
The bar is just set so low
For boys, most of you still are
Boring, so fucking played out with that tired game
I don't know how they get away with it
Doing so little to make a relationship work
Say something, ask a question at least
I know bitches like me are ruthless
But it didn't start this way
Future bating, juggling, distance and aloofness
Don't do it
Have a plan
Not an over-promise
It's lame as fuck.
Be direct and upfront
Red flags all over with repeated cycles
If you're still talking to your ex… nope
Take responsibility for your part
Unless you want to pay us for our time?
No? That's what I thought

The dickmatize wore off
All that's left is a sad puddle
We're all humans with needs, emotions
A two-way street
But damn, you ain't even trying
"Men at work" on your own path
Make peace with family patterns
Grow, evolve, admit wrongs
Love yourself over the ambition
Cause we tired of being ya chew toy
Ripped apart and replaced
By a new shiny toy every few months

Indirect Directness

I used to project you everywhere
Hoping to appear
In the 3-D
But what a fantasy
Years of back-and-forth got the best of me
We morphed and changed
But the toxicity stay the same
Just an echo of one night
What is a trauma attached site
Nothing ever really between us
As you could never open up
Promise me real thing
Instead of using me to end relationships
Always the third spike never the real one
If I could get you to admit your feelings
That would be hell frozen over
But I outgrew you
No false narratives
Or flattery could penetrate me
Not even for 30 seconds
Stalking me now is the only way
You can connect back
Looks like the spell reversed itself
And you're just trying to manifest me
Such a sad sack
Gaslit to keep me on some hook
Should have taken a second look
I grew faster stronger, hard make it
Look easy now, not like I've worked my ass of
Self flagellation with the truth it hurts

Gotta realize what didn't work
Fuck shit up inside my world
Now I am a different girl
Your lies and misdirects don't work on me
I'm all powerful miss Frankie
My sexuality is my weapon
Used against me all my life
I will destroy every last one of those men
By enjoying myself in private
Not a world or exclaim of such pleasure
Just to enjoy it with my choice of love
A real man who takes care of me
He is in tune with that inner nature
Aligned with the soul of me
I place my hand in his for safety
There I know I am free.

Merging Two Wolves

Virginally pure all in white
Can take her home
Show her off
Assured somehow she belongs to you
Cinderellie do the dishes
The housewife to cook and clean
Tend to your emotional need
The trophy, the prize
Always an appropriate size
Fits into that white couture dress
Never suspecting, but slightly suspicious
Of those girls she brags to
About the best man she knows
Oh all that glitters on the outside
While those eyes peer at Miss Lolita
Buxom and busting out
The slut that captures his attention every time
Leather and lace, whips and restraints
Just the thought makes his mouth water
Soul yearns for the complexity she brings
But what would the neighbors think
His family, oh daddy would not approve
The Ruffneck brothers
All sucking the same Kool-Aid
Sexualized, fetishized put in a box
Those women are just for fucking
Can't make a hoe a housewife
Who made her that in the first place?
Making her worship you on her knees
But she's the one who's really got the key

Madonna whore complicated
Complex division of what a woman could truly be
Separate to divide
Not one could surely compete
If we break them down into labels and brands
It's easier to buy their love
Rather than take their hand
Hold it and listen to know
A fully formed woman can do both
She is vast and deep as the Ocean
Her love could move a fucking mountain
Dominates the boardroom in the bedroom
Terrify the puritanical dregs of society
Old, shriveled ball sacks leading the charge
Trying to stuff an old fairytale
Back into flavor
For Eve and Lilith are one in the same
Something a man desires to control
But will only burn his hand on the flame
Goddess Kali stepped up to fight back
Face her wrath

Reversions

What if we kissed again
Under the neon lights
Late in the freezing night
What if instead of parting ways
Driving into icy fray
We came together again
Pressing your body into mine
Hand wrapped around my neck
Leg up thigh clicked into place
What if you weren't still wrapped up in your ex
That finally we might
Be comfortable to text
Sweet nothings too and fro
That emotional green light give a go
We could be lovers
Not just a cliff hanger of tangled emotions
Left hanging there to die
I promised to always love you
Unconditionally
Seems so open ended
Like we could have had a chance
So why not?
What you got against happy endings?
Afraid to do it all over again
Only outcome repeat if you don't learn
Time changes places
Faces become unrecognizable
But your soul is too familiar to leave
It's like a deep unmoved part of me
If I could truly let you go

That would be the end of me
This isn't my time to die
A fresh pressed start to mystify
Begin again and again and forever
The story is just at a climax
Baby lean back and just relax
Rollercoasters can be fun
Holding on to that ride or die no. 1

Shift of the Seasons

Darkness creeps
Howling wind upon the pane
Pain sinks into the bones
Slightly more brittle than before
A chill of hands and feet
Ghostly, ghastly thought might start to creep
The trembling trees
Kiss the browned leaves adios
Complex grays dot the sky
The mood of our city has shifted
A primordial creep of survival is knocking
Ratta tatt tatt
In Rhythmic order
Sanheim ritual is upon us
The greater the sacrifice of self,
The greater the reward
Where does the pattern stop
Here and now
Divert the path to something new
Don't hesitate or resist
Flag on the play
Foul begone to the depths of nowhere
Unwind your thread wormed into my spine
I am not a monster
Nor the robotic motion
I did not blister one too many times
Not to refuse it again
I am done with you rotten corrosion
Soiled the belief in my pure heart
Colored inappropriately the world
We are done here

Not bringing you with me
It must be declared
I will suffer no more from your games
Fool struggle
Not this insanity nor madness
Could bribe my stay
As it detaches from its stem
Once rooted firmly in the character flaws of me
It releases, without a care
Off into the sky
Perhaps fallen into the dirt or sewer
Degrading slowly into the mulches
For next springs flowers
Trusting that truth and the clarity
Buries seeds
The answers do come
Finally we see the point of it all
Reconciling the implosion it took
To finally get to stable ground
Knowledge gives freedom

Finding the End

Watching you slip away
Knowing I cannot change you
The love in my heart remains unchanged
Yet the physical distance becomes a bit longer
Never truly gone
Possibly never really here
Encapsulated in one pure moment
Yet we are more than moments
A collection of life's work
Some are golden
Breaking dawn upon an open valley of our awakening
Others are silent and still
After great and utter destruction
In between are the darkest of days
Laying sleepless in our bed
Wrinkled eyes from tears that poured
Wallowing in the regret of our foolish choices
Unable to understand how we one thought it was good
But you laughed and smiled
For one brief moment
Lifted out of such a misery of unsound choices
You looked into my eyes
Processing new and undiscovered information
Inquiring minds thought to know
I foolishly kissed your chest
My short stature leaving me in a disadvantage
Only able to dominate you in the bed
Your rejection was easy
I could not reach those lips
That which I was sure of
A supple kiss

Would awaken you from the deep slumber
Unbeknownst to you
That I was here, arrived in poor timing
To show you love
A feeling and simple action
Somehow had been miseducated
For it wasn't proof I needed, or you to perform
But a simple act of a kind hand
Reaching out to hold you
To reassure you of your place in this world
In mine
How glad I am
That you still live and breathe
Hoping that one day you will feel
Truly alive again

Baby Don't Hurt Me

Oh to love and be loved in return
Tales long and replayed
They just stick in your mind
Nothing will knock the feeling
I have to know what you're like
In every which way
Let me take care of the part of you
Unmanageable today
When I'm cold and sad
You'll sling your large coat over me
Hug me in really tight
Kissing my forehead
There will be challenges, no doubt
Life is a rollercoaster of nonsense
Unexpected fractures in reality
But I can make my way through
We can
I have faith in what we'll build
A team, in sync and ready to go
Your best friend
Equals
Fighting for this life together
Hand in hand
To be loved
And you know for sure you are loved
Must know in the heart
What love is
Loving you is loving me
You are worthy of the best
Accept the gift from the brightest of lights
Truth and clarity

A choice
To love and be loved
Giving of oneself
Over completely
No shield or guard
Sheer vulnerability and exposed arteries
Unpleasant parts that are still human enough
To be loved and love in return
A problem together tethers us
The long game
Inside jokes and tag teams
A thoughtful you is to me
Work out those tight muscle aches
Scratch a hard to reach itch
My love is more than imagined
As is yours
The love is all that is and ever was

Karmic Block

Gaslight, deflect
Don't bother with accountability
Just mean girl 101
I'll befriend you, just to get info on my man
Oh I'm just a victim of my circumstance
Participating in those power dynamics
Exclusion is women's greatest weapon
You're just my emotional dumping ground
For all the unprocessed bullshit in my head
As I go pose on some thrown
Get those perks of being with clout
Nothing I got for myself, but took willingly
Nothings ever free
Always a blood sacrifice to get something
Can't and won't even fight my own battles
I'll just dupe some poor sap into protecting
I believe this acceptable
Of course, I'm just an innocent in all that hurt you
Oh I can't decide, do I love you or not
I'll try a different guy in between
But he can't do the same
Inequity, inequality
Everyone is just a pawn in this game
Playing with people's kindness
Because I lack any of my own
I wanted to sit up on that thrown of swords
Like the dragon queen I project
Stealing bits of other's strengths
Taking theirs for weakness
Snakes in the grass aren't victorious
They just steal ideas as their own
Credit where credit's due bitch
Keeping people on leashes
You own no one and nothing
Not even your own dignity.

Free Range

In the quiet she roams
Peaceful in a tranquil space
The light, it pours down
Illuminating the shape of her
Fresh grapes glowing
The smell, intoxicating
Anything seems possible
Lying in wait to come into being
Vibrancy off of the molecules
All living beings, alert and instinctual
Gently buzzing in the air space
The hum of natural life going about
There is a harmony within
As so above and below
Beauty mixes and meshes
Fertile ground for future expansion
Dreams are just the beginning
A new chapter
The next season
Where it all happens
Believe in all notions
Big or small
An electrical current to nurture

Balanced with a hard line
Protect and deliver
Standing tall and unwavering
An external force
The commanding, calm, cool and collected
He is aware of all that surrounds
Merging the two paradigms may pose a challenge

Yet the interlocking pieces
Magnetically drawn
Could not be stopped
Raging impulse
Paired with a poised reception
How could he resist an invitation
In uncharted territories and unfamiliar terrain
Proceed with caution
For navigation may need translation
Plunged deep into the impacted waters of desire
A bit cooler, sound of the pulse getting louder
What do you want?"
"How hard are you willing to go?"
"What is stopping you?"
In the silence drowned state
Muted reality
The dire need is screaming
Gasping for air
Assessing
Act thoughtfully
Prosper
She takes one step
To begin a lifetime of new journeys

Disengage

My Counterpart
That's what he is
You might have trapped him
Thought you got a meal ticket daddy
Slipped him some mediocre slim nasty tounge
But my big daddy likes a fat ass
Kitty outside of the box
Independent thinker not a drinker
Someone who leads with positivity
Not a shit mouth or for brains
Bitch I got your number
Tick tick time is up
From the moment I saw you
Skinny as a bookmark
Disrespecting everyone around you
With an ugly ass mug
Masquerading as wife material
Hoe tales tell no lies
I ain't saying she's a Golddigger
But if the shovel fits
I'll bury you 6 feet under with my words
Do you want to test me
Drag names through the mud
You thought I was crazy
Loco mother fucking bitch
Trauma can shred even the biggest hearts
But mine
Is stronger than yours
My will alone can move mountains
I don't chase I attract
So let me school you this
Might've had them for a minute
But that boy is mine

Fucking and Fighting

How much do you have to suffer?
Self sabotage?
Resist and deter chances?
What is your control worth to you?
It's an illusion
There is no control
What you hold on to
Holds your head under water
Reality knocks and progresses
Even in your denial
If you died stagnating
What would that accomplish?
Grudges won't hold
Revenge unplayed out
If you stay the same
You're still carrying the burden
It owns you legally or not
Spiritually hooked into your heart
You've got options
A man of great talent and ability
Love so deep and devoted
The envy of all eyes
Be who you are meant to be
Success is your birthright
Loyalty is yours
Give yourself over to it
The grasp of white knuckles
Cannot sustain this storm
The electricity between us is stronger
But no one can give it a push

Harder than the universe
She punches with the might to destroy egos
The devil on the run
Whoosh
There is goes
Drop the baggage
Closure is a lie
It has come to pass
No more
Stop lying to yourself
Move on.
Fuck me or fight me
I can't take this much longer

The Release

It's time
To enjoy the ride
Flow with the tide
Live my dreams
A rebirth
Total lunar eclipse of the heart
I have to let go
My hand and my heart ache
It doesn't make sense anymore
Short lived and too late
Your lies are on display
The world knows your darkness
Devilish drama queen
You'll never change
Unlocked from this prison
Fuckery of epic failures
My abundance
The beauty and love await me
If I just let it in
I can't resist anymore
I want it
I need it
I have to have her
She is the one for me
The love of my life is here
Comparatively you are nothing
Abandoned ship with a broken bow
Sunken
I hope you get everything you deserve
What you've been dying for

Take your misery business
Controlling nature
You'll never change
But I have a new life
To prosper within
I see you
Ruined and seen by all
You are a disgrace
I am done
Done enough time
Can't stand it one second longer
Never again
I'm finally free.

Expulsions

You told me not to wait
Because of the pressure that position held
Full well knowing you had made me wait
All this time
Feeding a crumb of random information
Holding on to me, without intention
Disregarding the wake of chaos you left
The entanglement of our energy
Where you decided to choose someone easier
Woven anger into my heart
Sting of rejection bites harder that I could
Injustice of never having a true vulnerable talk
Failure on your part to see all the goodness that was me
A snippet of myself didn't flash campy enough
I wasn't manipulative
Not a player at heart
Dip my toes in just enough to leave prints everywhere
Just an alternative girl
With some scars and drive to find chaos
Desire mixed with pluck
Ambition to make the world hers
A black hole left from monsters
Those who begged for help
Only to steal her gold
I found your chaos, the madness leaking from you
Blind to any shred of reverberation
You moved through this world like no wrong could come
But you chose wrong
You fell far from grace
Huffing the pure bull shit of the gassed up ego
She was your kryptonite
Playing on your deep desire to be loved

Just a passing project picking you up
Like you picked me up all those year ago
I remember it well, the exact look in your eyes
Doubtful you could even process the memory
You're kind, but flawed
The delicious lie that is repeated
By adoring fan bases
Hidden frenemies
Those who know secrets and infer in posts
It all crushed the spirit
Chewed us up and spit out the bones
What a drug it is to believe
Grandiose thoughts of delusion
Fracturing ourselves into tiny pieces
Lighting self on fire to keep other warm
The sacrifice thought to bring great love in return
All it did was destroy the soul
We are not unalike
Yes, different creeds
Geographical space and familial curses
Operationally I know you
The story is my story
Your love is my love
So young and delusional we tried the only way known
The paths may deviate
But truly we are never alone
Never apart
It doesn't go away
Just becomes a faint cry into the darkness
Soul to soul
For ultimate combustion

The Truth

Always the girl who was your best friend
Yet never the one for a date
Not the first choice
Or even second and maybe third
A great listener of all your problems
With other girls
Overlooked and undervalued
As our value always seemed tied to the attraction of a man
I dated the weird and eccentric guys
Those who were oddly attracted to my difference
But still a lackey to their wills and desires
My first boyfriend dated me because I was nice
But also because the hot girl rejected him
Dumping me because a mean girl hated me
I watch guy after guy, date popular chaotic mess girls
Hoping to change them to be proper mates
Asking me the questions about what makes her tick
Sitting behind crush, after crush in class
Silently laughing at his entertainment for her
Wishing and hoping one day they would turn around and notice me
Intense and weird, the witch of every teen boy's nightmare
Always a good sense to run away from a player
Because I saw how they really treated women
I was never truly seen as anyone but a space filler
An acquaintance, the homely nice girl
Who somehow should do porn
Guys motives, confusing as they may seem
Were always clear
Unless you were fuckable, you didn't matter
Even intimately, they treated women as disposable
Who would want to date those guys anyways?
Why do you think pop-culture created an entire genre?

Trained us well
It was a man's world, but only the strong and over bearing
Everybody had to like whomever you were dating
Even if she was abusive and you hated her guts
The status of having some arm candy was undeniable
So many beautiful, smart and intelligent women
Never given their proper due
Sadly, I hoped to one day that I would be among the chosen
Validating all those little girl's ideas
Of how I was to be loved
No one pressed the idea to love yourself first
Always accepting, understanding, ever patient and never a complaint
One contrary statement
Oh, just a femme Nazi bitch from hell
So first I became void of space
Everything I thought he wanted
But still I was too much and needed to be beaten down further
Then I became larger than life
So that my energy would take up as much space as possible
I would become unsufferable, aggressive and make every man uncomfortable
They all had to be punished, right?
But it wasn't working
It didn't make me feel better
I had to undo and peel away every trope
All the lies and false beliefs about human nature
That we are all victims of a system that teaches us to hate ourselves
No matter how we exist it's always wrong
How they get us to buy shit
Keep us perpetually unhappy and overly motivated
To pursue what might make us slightly happier
So we men and women fight one another

Follow idiotic rules about conduct
Utter stupid phrases like Bros before Hoes
Chicks before Dicks
It's all a fucking lie
We see breaking through the matrix now
None of that truly matters
Because if we loved ourself enough
There would be no need to buy it
Restlessly seek it in shallow encounters
Fuck our way through people we don't even like
If we could just approach each other as equals
Speak truthfully about our pain
Not lead with a motive
Means to an end
Treating one another with respect rather than disposability
Perhaps we could end this cold war
And join together, within
To be loved and love in return

www.ingramcontent.com/pod-product-compliance
Lightning Source LLC
LaVergne TN
LVHW051040070526
838201LV00067B/4877